HARRIET ZIEFERT

Passover

Celebrating
Now

Remembering
Then

paintings by

KARLA GUDEON

BLUE APPLE BOOKS

Why is this night different from all other nights?

When we celebrate Passover, the youngest child asks the Four Questions:

Why on this night do we eat unleavened bread?

Why do we eat bitter herbs?

Why do we dip in salt water?

Why do we recline?

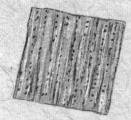

Why do we tell the Passover story year after year, time and time again? What do we remember?

We remember the Israelites lived peacefully in Egypt for many years until a new Pharaoh came to power. Worried that the Israelites would become plentiful, prosperous, and powerful, he forced them to become slaves, treating them harshly.

We remember when this cruel Pharaoh ordered all baby boys born to Israelites to be drowned, one mother refused and instead put her baby in a basket and floated it down the river.

We remember the Pharaoh's daughter found this baby and named him Moses, which meant, "drawn out of the water." She brought up Moses in Pharaoh's palace, but Moses never forgot he was an Israelite and that his people suffered greatly.

We remember when Moses saw a slave driver whipping an Israelite, he became so angry he killed the slave driver. Fearing he would be punished, Moses fled to the land of Midian, where he worked as a shepherd for many years.

We remember while tending his flock one day, Moses saw a burning bush, from which he heard the voice of God, commanding him to return to Egypt to free the Israelites. Moses returned to Egypt and demanded of the Pharaoh, "Let my people go!"

For Charlie and Lucy,
next in line to ask
the four questions
— H.Z.

For my loving family
who make every Passover
a musical extravaganza
— K.G.

Text copyright © 2010 by Harriet Ziefert

Illustrations copyright © 2010 by Karla Gudeon

All rights reserved / CIP Data is available.

Published in the United States 2010 by

Blue Apple Books, 515 Valley Street, Maplewood, N.J. 07040

www.blueapplebooks.com

First Edition

Printed in Dongguan, China 03/10

ISBN: 978-1-60905-020-7

2 4 6 8 10 9 7 5 3 1

Distributed in the U.S. by Chronicle Books

We remember the Pharaoh refused to free the Israelites and made their lives even harder. Time and again Moses pleaded with Pharaoh to free the Israelites; time and again Pharaoh refused.

We remember God told Moses to return and tell the Pharaoh if he did not free the Israelites, the Egyptians would suffer from plagues. But the Pharaoh would not listen.

We remember each time the Pharaoh refused to free the Israelites, God sent a new plague to the Egyptian people. With each new plague, the Pharaoh promised to let the Israelites go, but Pharaoh never kept his word.

We remember when God sent the tenth plague: the first-born male child of each Egyptian family would be slain. But the Israelites were commanded by God to mark their doorposts with the blood of a lamb so that the Angel of Death would pass over their homes, sparing their firstborn.

We remember when the Pharaoh's own son was taken, he finally agreed to free the Israelites. They rushed to gather their belongings, including their unbaked bread which didn't have time to rise.

We remember the Pharaoh decided he wanted his slaves back and sent his soldiers and chariots to follow them. When the Israelites reached the Red Sea, they were unable to cross, and with the Egyptian army close behind, they feared for their lives.

We remember Moses prayed to God and the waters parted, allowing the Israelites to cross the sea safely. But the roaring waters closed upon the Egyptians, drowning them all.

We remember that at last the Israelites were free, and so began their long journey, wandering in the desert for forty years, until they reached the promised land.

So that we never forget these events and the gift of freedom, we celebrate Passover and . . . we remember.

$\mathcal{N}$ow ...

We prepare the house.

We sweep.

We clean.

We remove the bread

and every last crumb.

Now...

We set the seder table.

$\mathcal{N}$ow . . .

*On the seder plate we place
the symbols of Passover.*

BEITZAH - roasted egg

KARPAS - parsley, celery, potato

Z'ROA - roasted lamb bone

CHAROSET - chopped apples and nuts

MAROR - bitter herb: horseradish root

CHAZERET - bitter vegetable: lettuce

MAROR

Z'ROA

BEITZAH

פסח

CHAZERET

KARPAS

CHAROSET

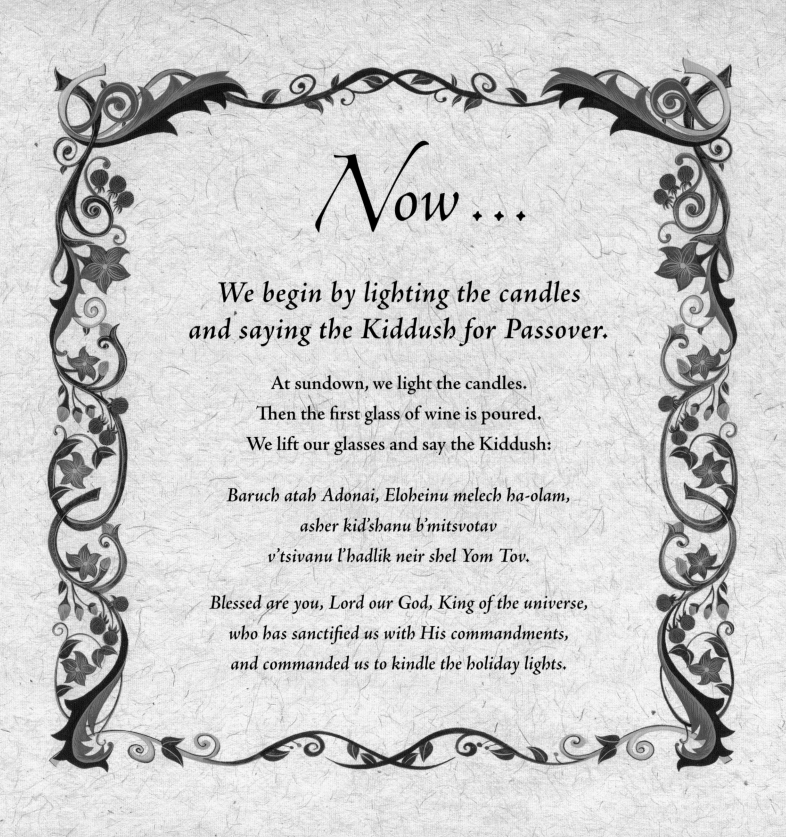

Now . . .

We begin by lighting the candles
and saying the Kiddush for Passover.

At sundown, we light the candles.

Then the first glass of wine is poured.

We lift our glasses and say the Kiddush:

Baruch atah Adonai, Eloheinu melech ha-olam,

asher kid'shanu b'mitsvotav

v'tsivanu l'hadlik neir shel Yom Tov.

Blessed are you, Lord our God, King of the universe,

who has sanctified us with His commandments,

and commanded us to kindle the holiday lights.

Kiddush Cup

$\mathcal{N}$ow ... ❖❖

We taste the parsley.

Parsley, potatoes, and celery
are symbols of springtime: new life,
promise, and hope.

Karpas

it was spring in ancient times.

Then...

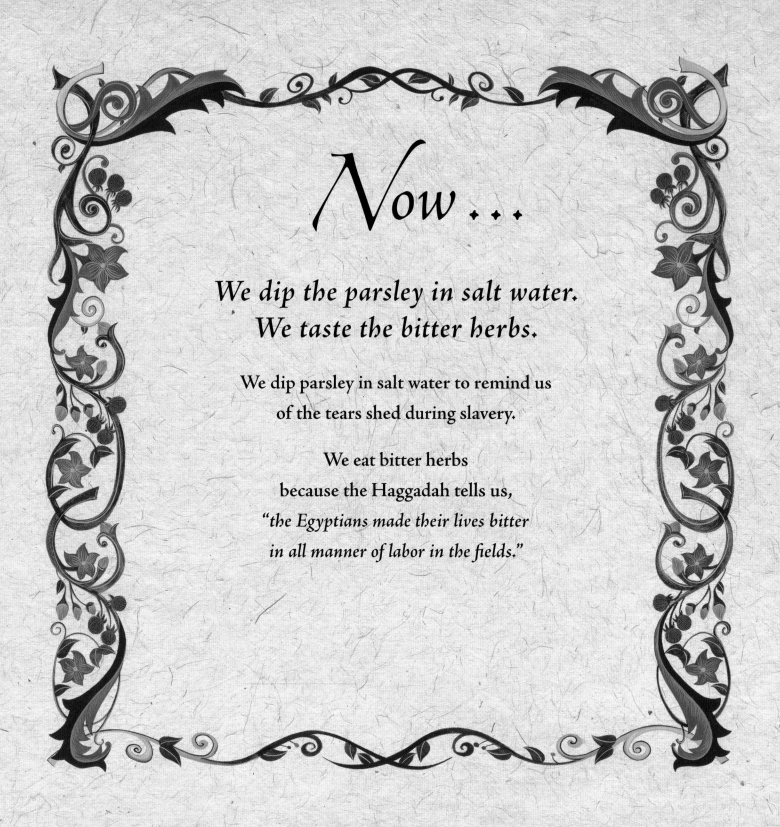

Now . . .

We dip the parsley in salt water.
We taste the bitter herbs.

We dip parsley in salt water to remind us
of the tears shed during slavery.

We eat bitter herbs
because the Haggadah tells us,
"the Egyptians made their lives bitter
in all manner of labor in the fields."

Dipping the Karpas

Maror

Chazeret

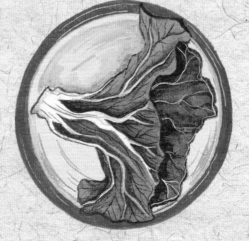

Then ... the Israelites labored as slaves in Pharaoh's fields.

Now...

We eat a mixture of
apples, nuts, raisins, and wine.

This mixture reminds us of the mortar
that our forefathers mixed as slaves.
Its sweetness represents
the promise of a better world.

Charoset

*T*hen . . .

Israelites were forced to make mortar
and bricks for the Pharaoh's pyramids.

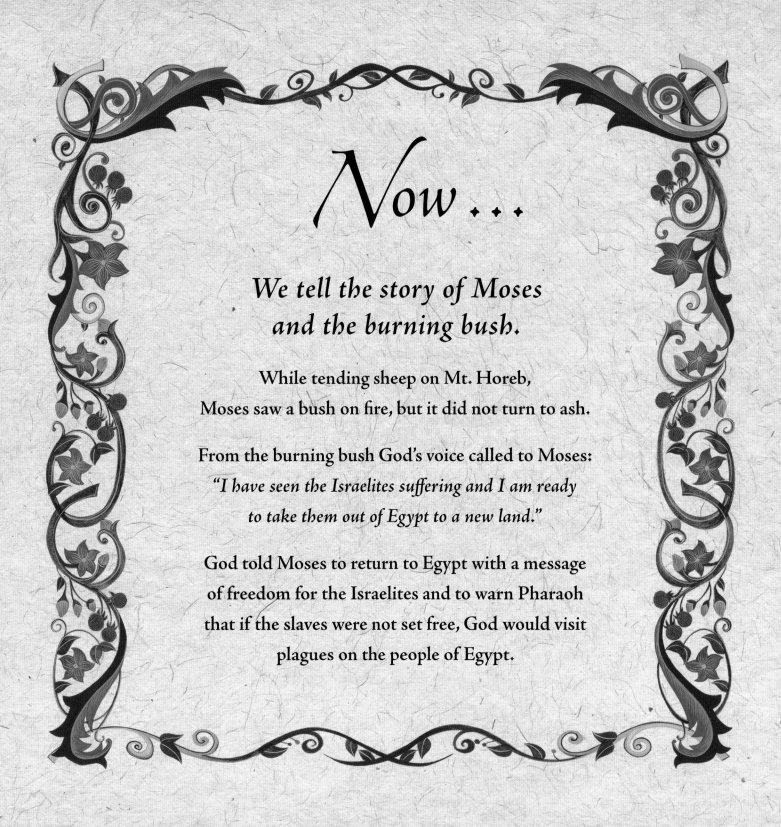

Now ...

We tell the story of Moses
and the burning bush.

While tending sheep on Mt. Horeb,
Moses saw a bush on fire, but it did not turn to ash.

From the burning bush God's voice called to Moses:
*"I have seen the Israelites suffering and I am ready
to take them out of Egypt to a new land."*

God told Moses to return to Egypt with a message
of freedom for the Israelites and to warn Pharaoh
that if the slaves were not set free, God would visit
plagues on the people of Egypt.

The Burning Bush

Then ...

Pharaoh refused Moses' request to let the Israelites go.

Now...

We drop ten drops of wine on our plates.

This reminds us of the ten plagues
that God inflicted upon the Egyptians.

BLOOD

BOILS

FROGS

VERMIN

BEASTS

CATTLE DISEASE

HAIL

LOCUSTS

DARKNESS

STRIKING THE FIRSTBORN

Ten Drops of Wine

*T*hen . . . God delivered plagues upon the land.

Now . . .

We hold up the roasted lamb bone.

This reminds us that before the tenth plague,
God told the Israelites to mark their doorways
with the blood of a lamb so that the Angel of Death
would know to spare their first-born children.

Z'roa

e Israelites.

Then . . . The Angel of Death passed over the homes

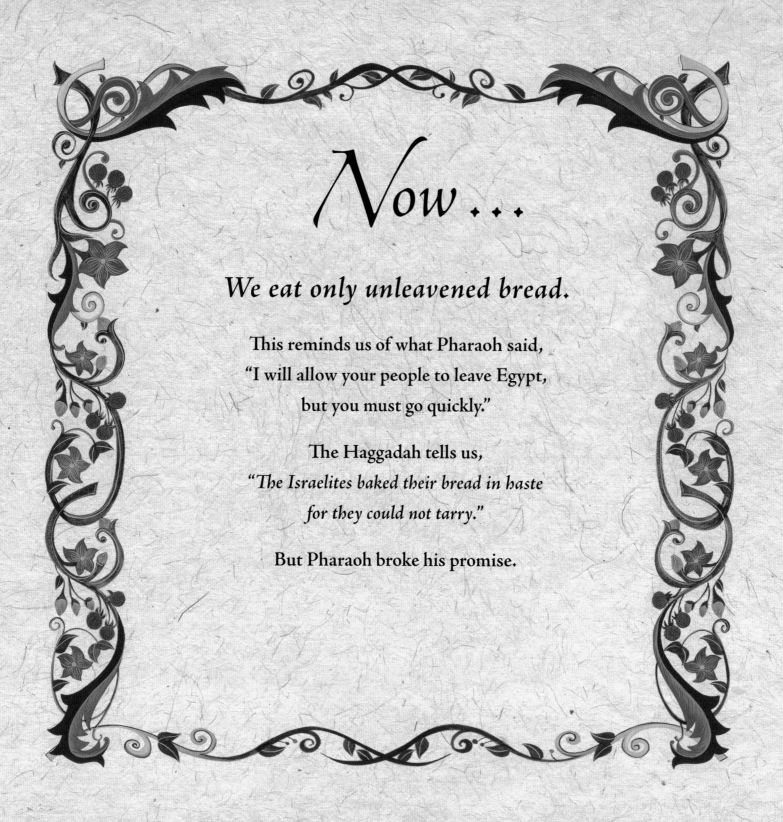

Now . . .

We eat only unleavened bread.

This reminds us of what Pharaoh said,
"I will allow your people to leave Egypt,
but you must go quickly."

The Haggadah tells us,
"The Israelites baked their bread in haste
for they could not tarry."

But Pharaoh broke his promise.

Matzo

Then...

The Egyptians chased the Israelites
through the desert to the sea.

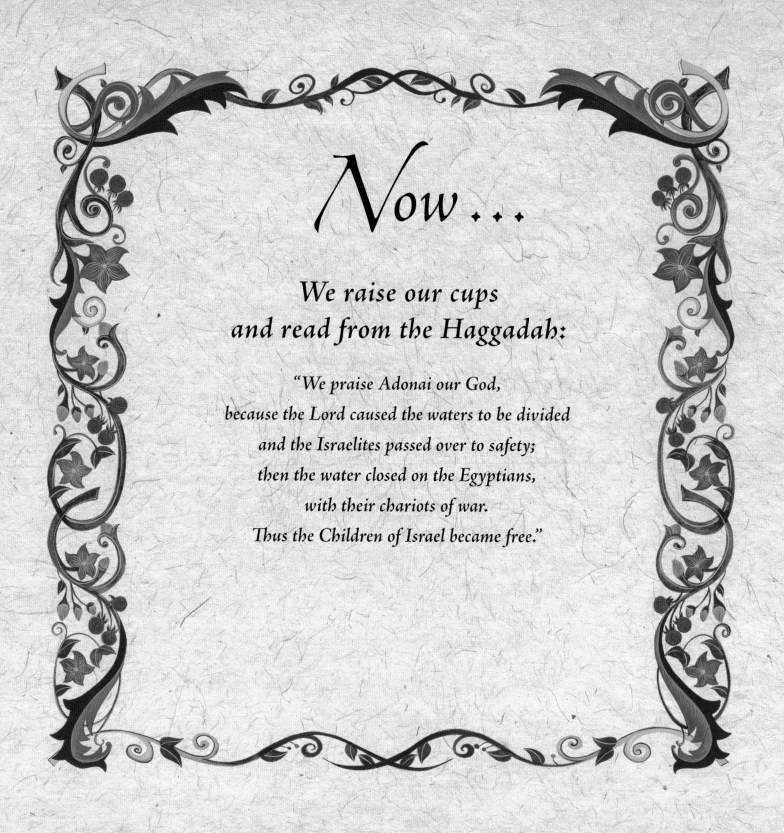

Now . . .

We raise our cups
and read from the Haggadah:

"We praise Adonai our God,
because the Lord caused the waters to be divided
and the Israelites passed over to safety;
then the water closed on the Egyptians,
with their chariots of war.
Thus the Children of Israel became free."

Passover Wine

Then...

The Red Sea parted
and the Israelites escaped their pursuers.

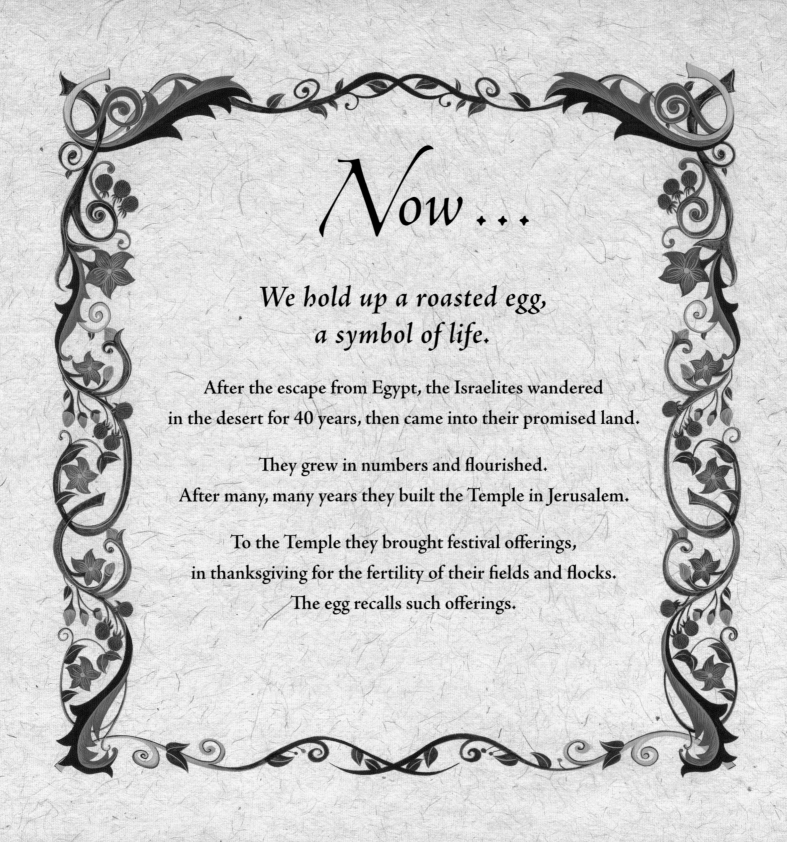

$\mathcal{N}$ow ... • •

We hold up a roasted egg,
a symbol of life.

After the escape from Egypt, the Israelites wandered
in the desert for 40 years, then came into their promised land.

They grew in numbers and flourished.
After many, many years they built the Temple in Jerusalem.

To the Temple they brought festival offerings,
in thanksgiving for the fertility of their fields and flocks.
The egg recalls such offerings.

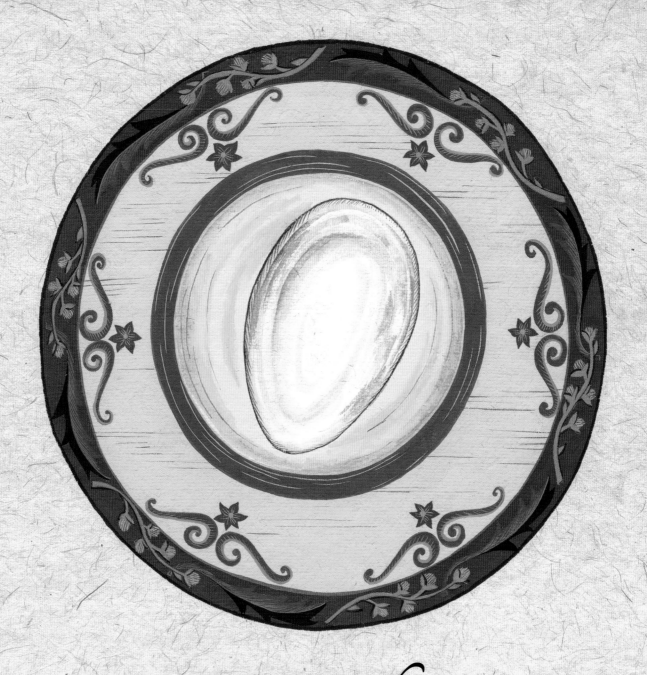

Beitzah

Then . . .

Israelites brought offerings to the Temple in Jerusalem.

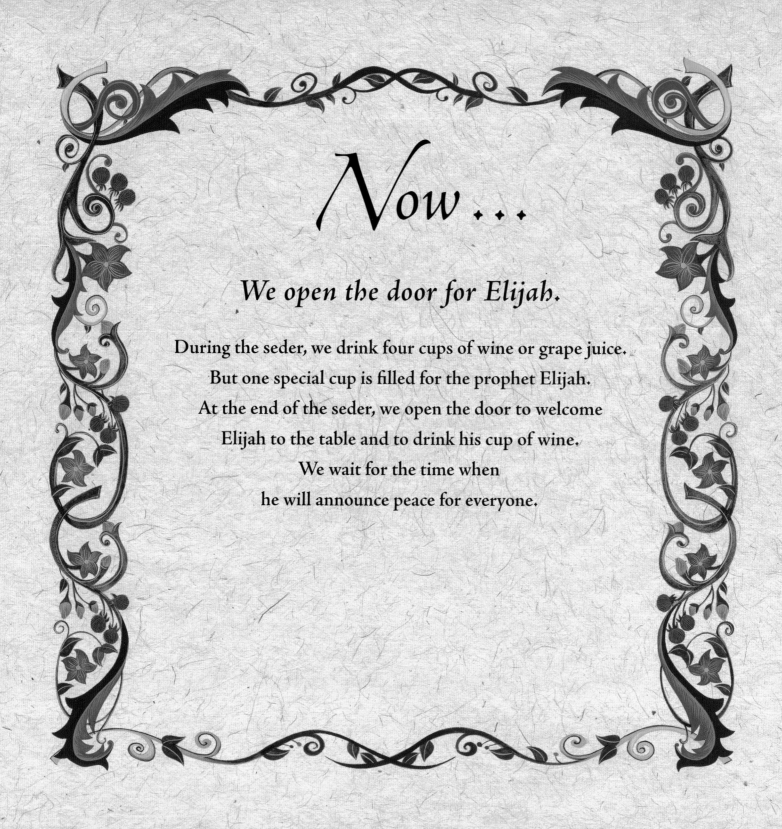

Now...

We open the door for Elijah.

During the seder, we drink four cups of wine or grape juice.
But one special cup is filled for the prophet Elijah.
At the end of the seder, we open the door to welcome
Elijah to the table and to drink his cup of wine.
We wait for the time when
he will announce peace for everyone.

Now...

We end the seder.

The children find the *Afikomen*,
a wrapped piece of matzo hidden at the start of the seder.
Once the special matzo is found, it is broken into pieces
and shared with everyone at the table,
so that the last taste of the meal continues to remind us
of the Israelites' liberation.

We sing songs to thank God for our freedom and end by saying,
"Next year in Jerusalem,"
which expresses the hope that all people,
all over the world, will be free.